Author's Dream

I dream of my India

- ➢ Which shall be an evergreen agriculture hub.

- ➢ Where no citizen suffers from hunger, starvation, and poverty.

- ➢ Where every farmer is happy, healthy, and prosperous.

- ➢ Where there are plenty of food supplies available and are distributed to the entire country at subsidized prices.

- ➢ Where no citizen, in both rural and urban areas, suffers from unemployment.

- ➢ Where the villages transform into towns and cities, which results in the decongestion of major cities.

- ➢ Where towns and cities shall have airports for better and faster logistics.

- ➢ Where our country earns huge foreign currency through its exports, which in turn makes our Rupee stronger than any other currency in the world. This is the only way to achieve this.

- ➢ Where agricultural business organizations shall adopt the social-business concept "Let's Grow Together." (*Sab ka Saath, Sab ka Vikaas*)

- ➢ Where all the people of our country are healthy, happy, and prosperous.

Om Namo Lakshmi Kubera Swarnaakarshana Bhairavaya

an idea of EVERGREEN REVOLUTION

(THE WAY TO SUVARN BHARATH)

CA.ASHEESH SESHADRI

ISBN 979-8-89233-513-3

Contents

CHAPTER 1

A Background of Agriculture in India Since Independence and its Importance

Agriculture is the most healthful, most useful and the most noble employment of Man.

— George Washington

India is demographically and geographically vast, socially plural, and culturally diverse.

With a population of 1.40 billion, India is the world's most populous country.

It is the seventh largest country in the world with an area of 3.2888 million square kilometers. It has a long coastline of 7,500 km.

India is a diverse country, where over 22 major languages and 415 dialects are spoken. With the highest mountain range in the world, the Himalayas to its north, the Thar Desert to its west, the Gangetic Delta to its east, and the Deccan Plateau in the south, the country is the home to vast agro-ecological diversity.

India is the world's largest producer of milk, pulses, and jute and ranks as the second-largest producer of rice, wheat, sugarcane, groundnut, vegetables, fruits, and cotton. It is also one of the leading producers of spices, fish, poultry, livestock, and plantation crops worth $2.1 trillion. India is the world's largest economy after the US and China.

India's climate varies from humid and dry tropical in the south to temperate alpine in the northern reaches and has a great diversity of ecosystems. 4 out of the 34 global biodiversity hotspots and 15 World Wildlife Fund's (WWF), Global 200 Ecoregions fall fully or partly within India.

Having only 2.4% of the world's land area, India harbors around 8% of all recorded species, including over 45,000 plant and 91,000 animal species.

For the financial year 2022, India was the world's fifth-largest economy by nominal gross domestic product (GDP) and the third-largest by purchasing power parity (PPP). Agriculture accounted for 19% of the GDP and employed 58% of the country's total workforce in 2022. However, India still has many growing concerns. As the economy has diversified and grown, agriculture's contribution to GDP has steadily declined from the years 1951 to 2011. While achieving food sufficiency in production, India still accounts for a quarter of the world's hungry people and is home to 233.9 million undernourished people. The incidence of poverty is now pegged at nearly 15%.

Agriculture, with its allied sectors, is the largest source of livelihood in India. Seventy percent of its rural households still depend primarily on agriculture for their livelihoods, with 86.2% of the farmers falling under the category of small and marginal.

While agriculture in India has achieved grain self-sufficiency, the production is resource-intensive, cereal-centric, and regionally biased.

AGRICULTURE: THE NEED OF THE PRESENT AND FUTURE GENERATIONS

I believe that there is an urgent need for this generation and also for future generations to attain an EVERGREEN REVOLUTION, which can set right the issues that are mentioned below:

➢ Our country being geographically and demographically vast, still, many people suffer from hunger, poverty, unemployment, and are deprived of basic health, too.

➢ 86.2% of the farmers in our country are small and marginal farmers. These farmers face continuous financial problems, which are explained in detail in Chapter 2. Due to these never-ending financial problems, their family lives are affected very badly in the areas of relationships, health, children's education, standard of living, social status, etc.

➢ Another factor is the underutilization of agricultural land due to various causes, like barren land, idle land, unproductive land, etc., which is explained in Chapter 3.

➢ And in contrast to the above, there is exploitation of agricultural land for real estate developments by big builders or corporates.

➢ Farmers and their children are migrating to urban areas for their livelihood. This is happening due to the continuous financial losses suffered by small and marginal farmers.

➢ Imports of many scarce/underproduced agricultural products affect our balance of payments (BOP) and foreign exchange earnings.

➢ A substantial section of small and marginal farmers, due to unsolvable financial losses, have resorted to being lazy and complacent by utilizing the benefits provided by certain Central and State Government schemes like the Mahatma Gandhi National Rural Employment Act (MGNREGA), etc.

> This is still an unorganized sector. There is a lack of professionalism in many areas like selecting the right quality seeds, timely crop protective measures, management of agricultural produce, etc. The management of agricultural produce is a big responsibility, which includes:

- What to produce, where to produce, how much to produce

- How to protect the produce during and after the harvest

- How, when, and where to sell.

> There is a threat from rich capitalists, who completely dominate and dictate the rules and policies, which benefit their businesses. And, incidentally, small and marginal farmers might be wiped off over a period of time.

> Soil repletion, overcoming groundwater contamination, regaining soil fertility, overcoming the causes of climate change and regional disparities, rectifying loss of biodiversity, sustainable agricultural production, efficient irrigation methods, and increasing the incomes of the farmers.

> The nation is yet to attain self-reliance (*atmanirbhar*).

So, to address all the above issues permanently, there is an urgent need to attain an evergreen revolution in our country.

I have conceived an idea to make our country attain an evergreen revolution. This idea, if implemented in its truest sense, in the right spirit, and in a scientific and disciplined manner, will really address the above issues and also provide plenty of benefits to various stakeholders of the country, namely the general public, farmers, youth, the country, investors, etc. This is discussed in Chapter 4.

These benefits are no ordinary ones but will make India a prosperous country perpetually and take care of future generations as well.

Readers Note

Readers Note

CHAPTER 2

The Indian Farmer: The Most Neglected Being

Let's not forget that the cultivation of the earth is the most important labour of Man.

When tillage begins, other arts will follow

The Farmers, therefore, are the founders of Civilization.

— Daniel Webster

We all know that food is a basic necessity for every human being to live. And the producer of food grains, vegetables, and fruits is the FARMER. It is because of the farmer that everyone has food every day and is alive, but still, he is the most neglected being, especially in India. He has not received the respect and support he deserves. The farmer suffers most of the time, and in a way, his sufferings have been perpetual. But people knowing or hearing this, just pity him, simply discuss the issue with others out of sympathy, and later forget. The ultimate truth and reality are that *nobody bothers or cares about the farmer*, neither the public nor the government.

The government proclaims that they have put a lot of effort and established initiatives, policies, plans, etc., to help and support farmers.

1. The government has established and is also in the process of establishing many agriculture research institutions, etc., and provides guidance to the farmers and supports the development of the agriculture sector, too, in many ways.

2. It provides financial assistance through the National Bank for Agriculture and Rural Development (NABARD), tax exemptions for agriculture income, subsidies for establishing any agriculture projects like sheep rearing, poultry, apiculture, sericulture, etc., and subsidies towards the purchase of agriculture assets like machinery, vehicles, etc.

3. The government has set a minimum selling price (MSP) for certain agricultural produce.

4. It conducts various educative programs for the farmers and provides training and continuous advice in various areas of agriculture.

5. The government waives the interest on loans taken by the farmers, and sometimes, even the principal amount.

Apart from these, there are many more initiatives by the government.

However, despite all the above aid, initiatives, policies, plans, and support from the government, the farmer is still suffering. WHY? We read news about farmer suicides almost every day across the country.

It appears very hard to accept the reality, and it seems ridiculous that, despite the above aid and support from the government, nothing much is actually benefitting the small and marginal farmers. Only the rich landlords seem to benefit.

THE PARADOXICAL POSITION OF FARMERS AND THEIR DISTRESSING LIVES

There is no guaranteed price mechanism available to farmers, and even if available, it is not properly implemented or executed, hence, the benefits barely reach the farmer. Thus, he always faces the brunt of the demand and supply mechanism, which destroys his returns irrespective of circumstances.

1. **Loss when there is bumper produce:** A farmer works day and night as required, and if nature and other factors favor him, he gets a bumper crop. Due to the limitations, like no guaranteed price mechanism, no proper storage facilities, and the financial burden of mounting interest on loans, he is compelled to sell the produce on the same day (in the case of perishable produce) or as early as possible (in the case of nonperishable produce) at a price dictated by the buyer (intermediary agents). This situation arises due to the demand and supply mechanism, i.e., the more the supply, the more the price falls. We observe this in our daily life where, sometimes, tomatoes or onions are sold for Rs.2 per kg. The farmer sells at a lower price when the situation dictates and suffers losses despite the fact he had a bumper crop.

2. **Loss due to involuntary and external factors:** Owing to various involuntary and external factors like heavy rain, drought, wind, infection, bad quality seeds, etc., the crop gets spoiled or become useless and the farmer cannot get a good price or even no price. In this situation, too, he suffers losses.

This is the paradox—whether he gets a bumper crop or loses his crop, he suffers losses.

One should try to understand what must be going on in their personal lives after these sufferings due to farming. They suffer financially, socially, mentally and health-wise also. Their family relationships are stressed, too, which impacts their children, makes their lives more vulnerable, dangerous, and in some cases useless. Sometimes, these circumstances may lead many to commit suicide. As per the data of India's National Crime Bureau (NCRB) for the year 2022, 14 farmers and 16 agriculture laborers committed suicide every day.

Imagine the scenario of our farmer, who is very hardworking and trusts God completely. And with a great hope and courage, he borrows money from financial institutions and any additional amount from moneylenders, pursues agricultural activity, and later suffers loss, which are inevitable—as explained in earlier paragraphs. The moneylenders brutally hound him. It becomes unbearable to face this and he starts worrying about it all the time. In order to forget, he might start drinking alcohol, for which he might again borrow money from his friends. When he goes home intoxicated, he gets into a fight with his spouse as she questions him or advises him not to get into this bad habit of drinking. In this intoxicated state of mind, having no self-control, he abuses or even beats her. These incidents, which happen every day, have a terrible impact on their children in many ways. Already, these families are suffering from poverty, live in unhygienic conditions, and are undernourished, which affects their health in the long run and negatively impacts the family.

Because of this state of affairs, the children may be forced to discontinue their education or, without proper guidance and care by their parents, lose interest in studies or fall prey to easy money and get onto the wrong path. Some children may go migrate to cities to work as construction laborers, security guards, cab drivers, etc.

Just observe how badly these families are affected. These situations are faced primarily by small and marginal farmers all over the country.

A very strange thing one should observe is that the government appears to be passive and negligent in finding a solution to the problems faced perpetually by these small and marginal farmers. Many a time, the governments, both Central and State, for the sake of vote banks, waive off the loans or interest or both of these farmers. One should understand that this is only a temporary solution. We need a permanent resolution whereby the farmers profit from their profession.

It appears that the governments neither have the required expertise nor the intention to diagnose the problem and provide the correct solutions. Instead, they provide temporary solutions, and the problems continue year after year.

Because of this attitude of our governments, the farmers are suffering perpetually and are the most neglected beings.

Readers Note

Readers Note

The Concept of Evergreen Revolution

Agriculture not only gives riches to the Nation, but the only riches she can call her own.

— Samuel Johnson

I will explain this concept for better understanding in five stages. Each stage comprises a group of activities/substages, which happen chronologically.

STAGE 1: FORMATION OF BASIC STRUCTURES

Substage 1: *FORMATION OF A BUSINESS ENTITY/ORGANIZATION*

Substage 2: ACQUISITION OF AGRICULTURAL LAND

Substage 3: FORMATION OF PROFIT CENTERS

Substage 4: PROCUREMENT OF FINANCIAL RESOURCES

STAGE 2: PREPARATIONS DURING PRE-AGRICULTURE PROCESSES / ACTIVITIES

Substage 1: *SOIL AND WATER HEALTH INVESTIGATION*

Substage 2: CHOICE OF APPROPRIATE AGRI PROCESSES

Substage 3: APPOINTMENT OF EXPERTS FOR EACH SPECIFIC AGRI PROCESS

Substage 4: APPOINTMENT OF EMPLOYEES FOR OTHER DEPARTMENTS

STAGE 3: EXECUTION OF AGRI PROCESSES

Substage 1: *CHOICE OF AGRI PROCESSES BASED ON SOIL AND WATER HEALTH REPORT.*

Substage 2: ADOPTION OF THE MOST SCIENTIFIC METHODOLOGY FOR EACH SPECIFIC AGRI PROCESS AND IMPLEMENTATION OF ALL THE STAGES (A to Z) RIGHT FROM TILLING OF THE LAND TO MAKING THE PRODUCE READY FOR SALE IN A PROFESSIONAL MANNER BY THE EXPERTS AND IN A TIMELY MANNER.

STAGE 4: POST-HARVEST ACTIVITIES

Substage 1: *STORAGE OF THE PRODUCE*

Substage 2: MARKETING OF THE PRODUCE

Substage 3: SALES OF THE PRODUCE

STAGE 5: GENERATING PROFIT AND SHARING

Substage 1: *GENERATING PROFITS*

Substage 2: SHARING AND DISTRIBUTION OF PROFITS TO VARIOUS STAKEHOLDERS

Let me explain all the stages and substages in detail.

STAGE 1: FORMATION OF BASIC STRUCTURES

Substage 1: FORMATION OF A BUSINESS ENTITY/ ORGANIZATION

- A legal business entity like a private limited company or a public limited company registered under The Companies Act, 2013, can be formed.

- Any government company, either Central Government or State Government, similar to Electricity Boards, Insurance Companies, etc., can be formed if any government wants to adopt this idea.

- A public-private partnership (PPP) model of a private or public company and the government can be adopted. The role of the company will be to bring huge capital and other resources like HR and expertise to execute the business and generate profits. The role of the government will be to help the company and contribute to the process of acquisition of land from farmers for the implementation of this idea.

- The company and the government may agree upon certain terms and conditions in all areas of this PPP, which is a win-win deal for both parties.

Substage 2: ACQUISITION OF AGRICULTURAL LAND

- The only mode of acquiring agricultural land for this idea will be on "lease rentals" as per the availing market price. I believe that the ownership of the land should always remain with the farmers and that this mode of lease rentals should be strictly followed. Any compromise/violation should not be tolerated and should be punished.

- The agricultural land should be acquired from small and marginal farmers and also from other farmers, if they are willing to provide it.

- Another strict rule is that "no land shall be taken by coercion/force". All the farmers have to come forward voluntarily to provide their land for lease.

- The company's founder/CEO/MD will have meetings with all the farmers in each village/taluk area. They should explain the idea and its benefits very clearly to various stakeholders in general and to the farmers in particular. A few more meetings should be held to explain all the processes for the acquisition of land with proper clarity by providing a road map.

- After the meetings, based on the understanding of this concept by the farmers, they should come forward voluntarily to provide their agricultural lands for lease rentals.

- This process of acquiring agricultural land from farmers for lease rentals can be simplified in the case of the PPP model or if the government, per se, wants to adopt it for their states or the country because the government's involvement gives the farmers more confidence.

Substage 3: FORMATION OF PROFIT CENTERS

- I will illustrate this with an example for better understanding.

- Example: Suppose an agri company acquires 5,000 acres of agricultural land in a village called Malgudi.

- Out of these 5,000 acres, each 1,000-acre parcel is created as a "Profit Center".

Profit Center 'A'	1,000 acres
Profit Center 'B'	1,000 acres
Profit Center 'C'	1,000 acres
Profit Center 'D'	1,000 acres
Profit Center 'E'	1,000 acres

- For each profit center, certain activities are centralized and some are decentralized. We have to thoroughly understand the various activities involved and their impact if centralized or decentralized and then decide.

- The purpose of forming a profit center is for:

  ✓ Better and healthy competition, amongst other profit centers

  ✓ Better management and implementation

  ✓ Better accountability and responsibility

Substage 4: PROCUREMENT OF FINANCIAL RESOURCES

- **Quantum of funding:** The quantum of funding shall be based on:

  ✓ **Nature of expenditure/cash outflows, i.e., capital expenditure and revenue expenditure/working capital.**

    - Capital expenditure is required for:

      1. Land and building for office, stores, administration, staff quarters, storage facilities

      2. Plant and machinery like agri equipment

      3. Vehicles for agriculture, e.g., tractors and other vehicles for plying the farmers and for transportation of the produce

      4. Software and hardware like computer software and systems, LAN, intercom, etc.

    - Working capital expenditure primarily includes, besides other working capital expenses, the entire costs of agriculture processes from start to end and contingent expenses like unforeseen costs like artificial cloud rain in case there is no rain.

✓ **Estimate the above expenditure for each profit center:** Estimate the above classified expenses for each profit center since each profit center has different and multiple agricultural activities.

For better understanding, let me explain through an example. Suppose an agri company decides to undertake five villages, which gives an average of five profit centers for each village. Each profit center may not indulge in the same kind of agriculture. For example, one profit center may cultivate paddy, a few others horticulture, sericulture, apiculture, poultry, etc. So, the funding should be estimated for each of the 25 profit centers based on their activities.

- **Who brings the funds?**

  ✓ Big companies like Reliance, TATA, Birla, Adani, etc., are capable of investing as they are financially capable and know how to run huge businesses in different sectors.

  ✓ Crowdfunding:

    - I visualize a "social-business concept" to be adopted, which is akin to crowdfunding.

    - The social-business concept gives the general public an opportunity to invest in the share capital of the agri companies. Through this opportunity, their money starts growing at a higher rate of return than in bank fixed deposits, mutual funds, or any other safe investments available.

    - The social-business concept gives every citizen of the country an opportunity, from the middle class, upper middle class, or lower class, to invest and grow their money, otherwise, only the rich and upper middle class people were able to encash these opportunities hitherto.

- The intention is to earn profits and share these profits with a larger section of society rather than a few individuals or rich people who already know how to make money.

- Also, if the idea of an evergreen revolution is implemented throughout the country, huge capital is required, and with this concept, every citizen gets an opportunity to invest and grow their money.

  For example, if Rs.1,000 crores is required for one village, a minimum of Rs.50,000 invested by around 2,00,000 people is sufficient

- Every investor gets a feel of actual ownership in that company as they will be legal owners or shareholders of the company.

- I have an acronym **FBO,** the full form being **FOR the People, BY the People, and OF the People,** to substantiate this social-business concept, which is an achievable revolution in this era where a capitalistic approach is ruling the world.

  FBO clearly explains that:

  1. There is a business investment opportunity **FOR** the People to utilize and grow their money by earning better returns.

  2. These investments shall be done **BY** the People

  3. **OF** the People's available money/savings, etc.

     To summarize, let the People sow the seeds and reap the benefits themselves.

- But, in order to make this social-business concept (FBO) successful, the business has to be managed in a very professional, transparent, innovative, and disciplined manner with complete accountability and responsibility.

STAGE 2: PREPARATIONS DURING PRE-AGRICULTURE PROCESSES /ACTIVITIES

Substage 1: SOIL AND WATER HEALTH INVESTIGATION

Soil and water are important components of sustainable agriculture. The overall health of these two ingredients plays a vital role in choosing what kind of agricultural activity one needs to engage in.

Soil quality does not depend just on the physical and chemical properties but is closely linked to the biological properties of the soil.

Based on the soil and water health report, only those parts of the land parcels that are suitable for crop production are utilized for that specific crop cultivation/production /horticulture, etc., and other parts of the land parcel are utilized for various other branches of agriculture like:

- ✓ Animal husbandry, which includes dairy farming and poultry farming relating to the rearing of chicken, goose, turkey, ducks, pigeon, Japanese quail, pork, rabbit, etc.

- ✓ Apiculture (bee rearing)

- ✓ Aquaculture (fish rearing)

- ✓ Sericulture and many other areas

Substage 2: CHOICE OF APPROPRIATE BRANCHES OF AGRICULTURE

The main purpose is to utilize the entire land parcel available for each profit center to its optimal use. It means that no part of the land parcel shall be kept idle or unutilized. It should be utilized for one or other branches of agriculture.

For example, assume a profit center of 1,000 acres. Out of these 1,000 acres, based on the soil and water health report, if only 400 acres are suitable for crop production or horticulture, then the balance 600 acres are to be utilized for other branches of agriculture.

Below is a diagram depicting the above example:

PROFIT CENTER (A) 1,000-ACRE LAND PARCEL

<table>
<tr>
<td rowspan="4">CROP PRODUCTION

OR

HORTICULTURE
(400 ACRES)</td>
<td colspan="3">ANIMAL HUSBANDRY

DIARY, SHEEP REARING, GOAT REARING, RABBIT REARING, CHICKEN POULTRY, GOOSE, TURKEY & DUCK POULTRY, JAPANESE QUAIL FARMING

(300 ACRES)</td>
</tr>
<tr>
<td>SERICULTURE
(100 ACRES)</td>
<td>APICULTURE
(50 ACRES)</td>
<td>HYDORPONICS
(50 ACRES)</td>
</tr>
<tr>
<td colspan="2" rowspan="2">AQUACULTURE
(75 ACRES)</td>
<td rowspan="2">ANY OTHER BRANCH OF AGRICULTURE

OR

RAINWATER HARVESTING, WASTE MANAGEMENT, ETC.

(25 ACRES)</td>
</tr>
<tr>
</tr>
</table>

For example, even if some part of the agricultural land is barren land that could not be utilized for any of the activities mentioned in the substage 1 paragraph, there will be a way to utilize this barren land for some use. I have read that in areas where water is scarcely available, palm trees can be cultivated as they need less or no water to grow. This vast knowledge is available in the world on agriculture as we have numerous agriculture research institutions across the world, agricultural educational institutions, and plenty of agricultural scientists and researchers. These resourceful think tanks can contribute with their vast experience, knowledge, and expertise to throw light on various issues or challenges that could be encountered and make this idea of an evergreen revolution a better and more successful one. This idea, as presented in this book, is only a framework, and anyone can make this idea more wonderful so that it can be useful to the entire world and its people, which can make this world a better place to live in.

Allocation of land parcels for appropriate branches of agriculture should be made based on the soil and water health report, climatic conditions, available resources, marketability, logistics, etc.

Once the allocation is finalized for that particular land and period, it should be strictly adhered to.

Some important aspects to be noted here are:

- Optimum utilization of the entire land of the profit center.

- Adopting a portfolio investment management strategy. (Don't put all the eggs in one basket) This strategy minimizes the risks, so, even if one branch of agriculture fails, then the other branches will be profitable and nullify or compensate for those losses.

Substage 3: APPOINTMENT OF EXPERTS FOR EACH BRANCH OF AGRICULTURE

This task is vital for the success of the operation. (Operations Risk Management Strategy).

Based on the various parameters like qualifications, practical experience, communication skills, management skills, etc., we have to select only EXPERTS for each branch of agriculture, who will lead from the front and be proactive in their approach.

Preferably, our own agri-scientists or retired or working agri-scientists from abroad should be recruited.

A more detailed scope of his work with roles, responsibilities, and timelines has to be discussed and they should adhere strictly to each branch of agriculture.

We have to support him/his services in terms of providing all the relevant, necessary resources for disciplined functioning in his area of operations. More specifically, care should be taken while selecting his team for the proper execution of his area of operations. We should collectively select the team.

Substage 4: APPOINTMENT OF EMPLOYEES FOR OTHER DEPARTMENTS

- ✓ **Appointment of laborers and supervisors for each branch of agriculture**

   The first preference for the employment of laborers, supervisors should be provided to the farmers, their family members, and relatives and only after that for others.

   They should be selected based on their age, experience, and skills.

   They should be recruited as permanent employees, not as casual laborers. They should be paid monthly salary and not wages, along with Provident Fund (PF) and Employees State Insurance (ESI) or medical insurance based on the salary. By doing so, they get the privilege of being a corporate employee.

   The most important aspect is ESI, which is akin to medical insurance for the lower salary bracket employees and will take care of the employees and their family members' health issues. Till now, they have been incurring these expenses themselves. This is very difficult as the medical costs are exorbitant, hence they find it unaffordable, and often, they lose their family members in case of critical illnesses or borrow funds from moneylenders, relatives, or friends and incur more debts and suffer drastically.

   People who need training should be provided the same and if any new technology has to be adopted, then proper training should be provided accordingly.

The company/organization will have the liberty to shuffle/shift the employees from one profit center to another or from one village to another.

The best thing that happens here is that all the people in the villages will get employment opportunities.

✓ **Appointment of employees for other than fieldwork**

Employees for other departments have to be recruited in a professional manner.

STAGE 3: EXECUTION OF THE PROCESSES IN EACH BRANCH OF AGRICULTURE

This involves adopting the most scientific/successful methodology, implemented professionally by the EXPERT and his team in a timely manner at every stage/process (A to Z) in their respective branches.

Let me explain by the example of the stages of paddy crop production:

1. **Preparation of the field:** Paddy farmers get their fields ready before the rainy season. The weeds are cleared, and the field is plowed by buffaloes or tractors to a depth of a few inches.
    Manure and fertilizers are added to the soil.
    The whole surface then remains covered with about 2.5 cm of water.
    The field is then ready to receive seedlings from the nursery.

2. **Transplantation:** Generally, paddy seedlings are first prepared in the nursery. The transplanting is done in the field after 40 days.

3. **Field maintenance:** Paddy fields require regular maintenance, such as occasional weeding and thinning out the more crowded patches. The level of water to be maintained is according to the growth, and fields are drained dry before the crop is harvested.

4. **Harvesting:** The traditional harvesting system is either through a curved or sharp-edged knife.
    It is very labor-intensive.
    Harvesting is done in the dry season when the weather is sunny.
    Mechanical combines that cut and thresh can be used.

5. **Threshing, winnowing, and milling:** After the paddy stalks have been gathered and dried for a brief spell, threshing is usually done by beating the sheaves against the bars. The grains are separated from stalks. Nowadays, threshing machines are available.
    Winnowing is a process of removing unwanted particles from the paddy grains. The simplest way is by pouring the paddy down

from a height on a windy day onto a large square mat on open ground. The grains fall onto the mat while the lighter chaff blows out. Sometimes, hand winnowing machines are also used.

Milling means removal of the yellowish husks from paddy so that white or polished rice is obtained. In a rice mill, the paddy is made to pass between varying sets of hullers or rollers till it is milled or polished

After the final produce is ready to sell, the other departments' roles begin, like packing, storing it properly and safely, and transporting it to godowns or the place of sale.

STAGE 4: STORAGE, MARKETING AND SALES, WASTE MANAGEMENT:

There is nothing much to explain about the roles and responsibilities of these departments as their functionality is akin to the departments of other FMCG companies.

But a few points need to be noted:

a. We should provide sufficient storage facilities for all branches of agriculture we practice in each profit center or each village.

b. The marketing and sales departments are advised to concentrate both on national and international markets.

c. Waste management can be innovative to convert waste into revenue or reusable resources like manure, *gobar* gas, etc.

STAGE 5: GENERATING, SHARING, AND DISTRIBUTION OF PROFITS:

By adopting scientific methodology, a systematic and professional approach, acting in a timely manner, adopting the latest technology in machinery, equipment utilization, and crop production enhancement, and using advanced biotechnical inventions/discoveries these profit centers can produce abundant produce in each branch of the agriculture we practice, and with the help and support of professional, experienced teams in marketing and sales, they should be able to generate excellent profits.

An important point to be conveyed here is that 20% to 25% of the profits should be shared with all the farmers who have given their lands on lease to the company in proportion to the individual land given to the total land given for that particular profit center.

Example:

Farmer A has leased two acres of land.

Farmer B has leased land one acre of land.

The total land acquired on lease for profit center A is 1,000 acres.

The profit earned is Rs.50 crores.

Here, the farmers are eligible for 25% of the profits in the proportion of their leased land to the total land leased for that profit center.

Farmer A gets 25% * Rs.50 Crores * 2 acres/1,000 acres = Rs.2,50,000

Farmer B gets 25% *Rs.50 Crores * 1 acre/1000 acres = Rs.1,25,000

The remaining 75% of the profits should be available for the shareholders, which could be distributed as dividends or reinvested.

Conclusion: I want you to envision how, if the entire country adopts this model and the entire agricultural land is used to its optimum, what the benefits available to various stakeholders like farmers, the general public, villages, cities, the country's food production, foreign exchange earnings, and shareholders' return on investment (ROI) can be.

Secondly, this model requires more financial capital, which can be easily achieved by the FBO approach of making every interested citizen an investor in these organizations in whatever capacity he can.

For example, the ticket size of investment in the share capital of these companies or organizations could be a minimum of Rs.25,000 to a maximum of Rs.10,00,000 per investor.

Imagine, if at least 40% of the eligible population invests directly in these companies or organizations...

The population of India in 2023 is 143 crores.

Let's assume that the people eligible for investment are 90 crores, the non-eligible being children and non-earning individuals.

40% of a 90-crore population is 36 crore people.

On a conservative assumption, if the average investment is assumed to be Rs.1,00,000, then capital availability will be Rs.1,00,000 * 36 Crore people = Rs.36,00,000 crores which is almost equal to 75% of India's Union Budget 2023–24.

Readers Note

Readers Note

CHAPTER 4

The Benefits to Various Stakeholders

Agriculture is our wisest pursuit, because it will in the end contribute most of real wealth, good morals and happiness.

— Thomas Jefferson

I firmly believe that, through proper implementation of this idea of evergreen revolution throughout the country, there is a definite opportunity of deriving enormous benefits for various stakeholders and we can achieve the status of "Suvarn Bharath" or "Golden India".

The stakeholders, who will benefit from this idea have been classified broadly as (1) farmers (2) the general public and the nation (3) shareholders/investors.

1. **Farmers:** Farmers play a pivotal role in the entire agriculture process of the country. I started thinking of a solution for farmers when I began empathizing with farmers and their circumstances and listening to and reading about their suicides in the news. I designed this idea in such a way that I have given

more importance and provided multiple benefits to the farmers, who have been the most neglected ones.

Benefits:

a. **Lease rental income:**

- As explained earlier, the agri companies or profit centers should acquire agricultural land parcels only on a lease rental basis.

- The lease rentals should be fixed at a price that is not less than the market price prevailing in that area along with an escalation clause of 5% to 10% every year in the agreement between the agri company and the farmer.

- This lease rental will be one of the sources of income for the farmer. Of course, though this income will not be a substantial amount for small and marginal farmers, they will earn a fixed income every year.

- As the ownership of the land always rests with the farmers, their land goes on appreciating gradually, which is like long-term capital appreciation as their lands are used optimally and the demand for the agricultural land will increase.

b. **Share in profits earned by the agri company/ profit center:**

- As explained in one of the earlier chapters, a minimum of 25% of the profits earned is to be shared proportionately in the ratio of the land provided to the profit center/agri company to the total land provided to the profit center/agri company.

- This is another source of income for the farmer.

- Besides the income, it gives the farmer privilege and pride as he will be a shareholder/part owner of that profit center/ agri company.

c. **Employment in agri company/profit center:**

- A monthly salary income, akin to that of a corporate employee, should be provided.

- This income will provide them with financial security to live their daily lives happily.

- I recommend a monthly instead of daily/monthly wages deliberately to incorporate two important aspects—health and retirement benefits.

- As we know, "health is wealth", but for this generation, the quotation changes to "Health is MORE than Wealth." So, this is an important factor as poor farmers will not be able to bear the health costs. Hence, we need to provide Employee's State Insurance (ESI) or Group Mediclaim Insurance according to the applicable laws available.

- Retirement benefits are also very important for the post-retirement life of farmers and other employees. Pension should be accommodated through Provident Fund, superannuation, or gratuity schemes.

- So, with these, we have tried to take care of our farmers fairly in a comprehensive manner.

2. **Benefits to the general public and the nation:** I believe that agriculture is the most important industry that can make our nation self-reliant and prosperous. If a substantial section of the population shifts its focus to agriculture, the general public and the nation derive many benefits:

   i. **Zero unemployment:**

      a. **Employment for farmers:**

         - Most farmers and their family members will be employed in the agri companies/profit centers.

- All the youth in villages, other than farmer families, will have employment opportunities or other entrepreneurial opportunities.

- Training, if required, should be provided to those who are new to farming. Also, whenever any advanced or new techniques are adopted, training for all should be provided.

- Hence, most of the people in the villages will get employment according to their education, if any, or experience and interest in particular agri processes.

b. **Employment for the general public:**

- Once the corporates, set up their businesses in villages in a big way, the organizations need all the other departments like HR and admin, accounts, cost, purchase/procurement, hardware and systems admin, marketing and sales department, transportation and logistics, fixed assets management, R&D, soil and water conservation, stores, cold storage, employee welfare, and many more.

- There shall be enough employment opportunities available to all the graduates, post graduates, research scholars, scientists, specialists of agriculture discipline.

- The general public gets many employment opportunities according to their educational qualifications, experience, etc.

- Imagine if the entire country adopts this idea and the entire agricultural land is utilized, then this will create a great number of employment opportunities, and I strongly believe there is a certainty that the country can achieve 100% employment for all our citizens.

ii. Business and other opportunities

- Once corporates set up business hubs in villages and many people get employment, these will consequently create several business and other opportunities like:

- Agriculture business opportunities: Agro-based industries, cold storage facilities, agri-machinery manufacturing businesses, shops/establishments, agri-machinery or tools rental businesses, etc., will emerge due to the requirements.

- Real estate opportunities: As more people get employed in these companies, people will migrate from cities/towns. Being used to city culture, they will need homes, schools, and colleges for their children, hospitals, entertainment hubs like malls, cinema theatres, eateries/food courts, lodges, hotels, fuel stations, vehicle showrooms, etc., and these villages will get converted into towns or smart cities. There will be extensive construction activities which will fuel further employment opportunities.

- Educational institutions: Here too, the construction of buildings/infrastructure is needed. Employment opportunities will emerge for the complete functioning of the schools, colleges, etc.

- Health care and hospitals: Employment opportunities will emerge for the complete functioning of these facilities.

- Entertainment hubs: Employment opportunities will emerge for the complete functioning of entertainment hubs like malls, food courts, pubs, hotels, lodges, clubs, etc.

- Transportation/logistics: Employment opportunities emerge for the complete functioning of these departments for corporates and many small and medium entrepreneurial business opportunities. There will be huge requirements for transportation and logistics for the movement of people from various locations to the sites, from cities to the corporate offices, the movement of goods, agri produce from the fields, or other places to the factories, industries, etc., and to the storage hubs and sale locations. For example, groundnuts are moved from the field to the factory to remove the outer shell. From there, they are transported either to the oil mills for oil extraction or to the purchasers' locations.

- I am optimistic that, over a period of time, due to the potentiality of the businesses, particularly agri produce, even airports will be required and established so that the agri produce can be directly exported to other countries from these towns that were earlier villages. Many other incidental opportunities will emerge...

iii. **The growth of villages to towns and decongestion of cities**

- As explained earlier, because of several employment opportunities emerging, people, in general, will migrate from cities to these places, and more particularly, people who had earlier migrated from villages to cities for work or employment will return. Once people vacate cities, cities will get decongested and the air quality will improve. Besides, these villages will get converted into towns or smart cities as more urban people settle there.

Of late, there is a lot of infrastructure development across the country, particularly laying good roads, like toll roads by the National Highways Authority of India (NHAI), which gives better connectivity, safety, and ease of traveling in less time. This will help people to commute to villages on weekdays and spend weekends in nearby cities till most of the facilities are made available in the villages. Some may even travel daily from cities to the offices in company transportation.

iv. **Food subsidies for the entire nation**

As we will be able to generate surplus produce from every agricultural activity, the agriculture companies can either give a certain percentage of their output to the government for free or at a subsidized price so that the government can provide subsidized food grains to the entire population.

v. **Substantial amount of foreign currency earnings through exports**

- A lot of R&D is happening continuously across the country and the world in the field of agriculture by various private and government research organizations. Most of the R&D focuses on how to improve yield substantially. For example, 5X, 10X, etc., for the given land area. This will help farmers to get more yield in small parcels of land and earn more revenue.

- In hydroponics, an Israeli technology where plants grow in water, there is no requirement for soil. Here, mostly horticulture or floriculture can be implemented. The main advantage is similar to the above—that within a small piece of land, they adopt vertical farming, which improves the yield by 5X to 10X depending on the crops. Secondly, they can have six harvests a year, which is a straight 6X.

- So, ultimately, any technique or research output that fetches us more yield should be adopted. We can then produce huge quantities of agri produce in various processes of agriculture. If the whole country adopts this concept and methodology, there can be substantial food grains, vegetables, fruits, etc., where we can provide food subsidies to the entire population of our country and even export to other countries.

- Besides food grains, there is a huge market abroad for various items like horticulture produce, where specially grown exotic vegetables, exotic fruits and greens (leafy vegetables) are in great demand in European countries.

- Meat is also in great demand, besides beef and other meats, rabbit meat, Japanese quail eggs (these eggs and meat have medicinal value and are recommended by doctors for paralysis patients), pork, sea food etc.

- Spices and other expensive items.

- Once the entire nation adopts the EGR idea, we can produce qualitatively best and quantitatively abundant produce and export them, which will fetch the nation abundant foreign exchange earnings, which will help to reduce/wipe off balance of payments and also make our rupee stronger in the world. We can achieve the dream of our many leaders of making ₹1 = $55 happen.

3. **Benefits to shareholders/investors:**

This being a social-business concept, which over a period of time spreads across the entire country, obviously requires huge capital.

There is a huge opportunity for all the citizens of our country to invest and grow their money.

Ultimately, an investor looks for higher ROI. In this case, the internal rate of return (IRR) cannot be less than 12%, which is more than bank fixed deposits or any other safe investments available in the market.

Also, with this concept, the company can take advantage of the various loans and subsidies provided by the government besides the equity.

I wish to emphasize the point that every investor will get the privilege of being a shareholder—a part owner/co-owner of the company. Being a shareholder, the risk as well as return is spread across other investors. This investment, too, qualifies as a safer one as there are regulatory authorities like the Security and Exchanges Board of India (SEBI), the Companies Act, 2013, and many more, which safeguard investors and funds.

The investor has multiple choices of investing in any company or profit center across the country. He can adopt the portfolio investment technique and invest across various companies (not keeping all his eggs in one basket).

Readers Note

Readers Note

Probable Challenges/Risks Arising in Each Stage and How They Can Be Addressed/Mitigated

If agriculture goes wrong, nothing else will have a chance to go right.

— M.S. Swaminathan

The title of this book, *An Idea of Evergreen Revolution*, involves two important words—"Evergreen" and "Revolution".

First, let me speak about "Evergreen". It means having an enduring freshness, success, or popularity. In other words, it means perpetual, everlasting, or never-ending. To make anything perpetual is very difficult as it involves a lot of challenges or risks that should be addressed or mitigated by discovering possible solutions. Discovering the possible solutions has to occur by analyzing the challenges based on various parameters, and always adopting a win-win strategy.

The word "Revolution" as per the *Oxford Advanced Learner's Dictionary* means "a great change in conditions, ways of working, beliefs, etc., that affect large numbers of people." This new idea has to be adopted instead of the existing systems, not by ignoring them completely but with major modifications required to achieve our goals as envisaged in the previous chapter on benefits to various stakeholders.

Adopting a new system is not easily acceptable to anyone. Basic human nature is resistant to change. In order to convince the public, we should perform and prove through a pilot project and show them the potential of this concept and its benefits to many stakeholders.

Whenever a perpetual new system has to be introduced and practiced, obviously there will be various challenges to be addressed and risks to be mitigated, intelligently and innovatively. Unless we address these challenges and risks head-on, we will have feeble chances of moving forward.

I have identified certain challenges/risks in each stage of the idea implementation and suggest a few solutions/measures to address them.

In all humbleness, I accept that the challenges/risks and the measures suggested below might be limited to my thinking or vision and request rather invite the general public, scholars, scientists, agri experts, etc., to analyze this idea and visualize other risks/challenges and also suggest great solutions to make this a wonderful idea and make it possible and successful practically so that it will be beneficial to mankind and society. I do not claim any finality for the views expressed in this book.

Let's explain below the challenges/risks involved in each of the stages of the idea and the measures or solutions to address/mitigate them.

STAGE 1:

Substage 1: FORMATION OF A BUSINESS ENTITY / ORGANIZATION

The selection of an organization could be a private limited company, public limited company, or limited liability partnership (LLP). It could be a separate entity for each profit center or for a group of profit centers—approximately 25–30 profit centers. It is better to incorporate one organization for multiple profit centers as the incorporation costs, the Companies Act, 2013, compliances work and costs, and many more administrative works and costs can be saved.

The important aspects to be considered while selecting are:

- The number of people to be accommodated as shareholders.
  For example, a private limited company can accommodate a maximum of 200 persons as shareholders. But there is no limit on shareholders for a public limited company.

- Tax benefits, savings, and concessions available to a particular sector/company/organization.

A small thought: If this idea is adopted by the country substantially, then we can request the government to provide additional benefits like:

- Direct/indirect tax concessions to the companies and individuals who have invested on their investment income and also on farmers' earnings.

- Enhancement in the amount of already available subsidies or additional subsidies.

- Easing the procedures of land acquisitions and others.

Substage 2: ACQUISITION OF AGRICULTURAL LAND

- The major risk would be a delay in acquiring the agricultural land if the land has to be purchased. But here, we are supposed to acquire these land parcels for LEASE RENTALS only for a period of 20–25 years or more as per the market rates plus an incremental increase of 5–10% every year.

- We have to make the farmers understand this idea in its entirety—its benefits to them and their families—and also to other stakeholders. This can be done, first, by arranging meetings with the village heads, MLAs, MPs, etc. and explaining to them clearly and seeking their continuous support/cooperation to become intermediaries to bridge any differences between the farmers and the company.

- Also, state governments or the Central Government can support this concept by being a party to the Lease Agreement. It should be a tripartite agreement.

> **Farmers leasing land to ⟶ Government ⟶ subleasing land to ⟶ Agri Companies**
>
> **Agri Companies pay lease rentals to ⟶ Government ⟶ pays lease rentals to Farmers**

- If the government becomes a party, the farmers feel more secure and gain more confidence, and the process of acquisition can be faster and easier.

- Farmers granting their agricultural land for lease should be absolutely voluntary and not compulsory.

Substage 3: FORMATION OF PROFIT CENTERS

- As per our concept, we have considered the profit centers will be a cluster of 1,000 acres or more of agricultural land parcels.

- The cluster of 1,000 acres may not be in one place or continuous land because some farmers may not be willing to give their land for this idea, and hence, the acquired land may be in a haphazard manner.

- So, we have to clearly mark/fence the boundaries of the profit centers to avoid future problems and for better clarity for both parties.

Substage 4: PROCUREMENT OF FINANCIAL RESOURCES

The main challenge is to build investor confidence.

This can be done by explaining the benefits and how his funds can be safe and earn higher ROI.

- Privilege of being a shareholder

- Both risk and return are shared

- Methods/strategies employed to increase the profits

- The social-business concept, "Let's grow together" akin to *"Sab ka saath, sab ka vikaas"*

STAGE 2:

Substage 1: SOIL AND WATER HEALTH INVESTIGATION

Substage 2: CHOICE OF APPROPRIATE AGRI PROCESSES

- Initially, it is better to send the soil and water for their health reports to reputed laboratories for accuracy.

- Later on, we can have our own in-house laboratories and get the soil and water tested there professionally.

- Soil and water health reports are vital for selecting amongst the various branches of agriculture, which ultimately depends on the profitability of the profit centers.

- There is no risk, particularly where the soil and water health report favors typical crop production. But there is a risk in choosing the right branches of agriculture for the remaining land parcels where no crop production is possible. The right choice has to be made considering various factors like climatic conditions, feeding raw materials availability, transportation, readily available market, availability of experts, veterinary doctors, etc.

- Once the right choice is made, then, implementing all the other stages in a professional manner will make it successful.

- This is a very vital step as it is akin to a portfolio investment management strategy. Here, we invest our land and financial resources in different agri branches based on the soil/water health report. The success of the entire profit center is dependent directly on the decision to choose different branches and implement them accordingly.

Substage 3: APPOINTMENT OF EXPERTS FOR EACH SPECIFIC AGRI PROCESS

- The challenge here is to select the right candidate who is an expert for that particular branch of agriculture. For example, experts on paddy cultivation, floriculture, etc.

- The risk is that the success of the chosen branch lies in his abilities and expertise.

- Besides his qualifications and experience, he should be proactive and innovative in his approach. We cannot hire people who are reactive.

Substage 4: APPOINTMENT OF EMPLOYEES

- The challenge here, too, is to select the right candidates for each department.

- Candidates who are willing to migrate to villages should be preferred/selected, because, without a willingness to stay in rural areas, there can't be effective productiveness.

- In order to attract people to villages, the challenge also lies in making the environment more appealable as is available in a town/city by providing all the facilities for them and their families so that they may show a willingness to migrate. This means providing good educational institutions, transport systems, medical facilities, good internet connections, entertainment centers, etc.

- Internal control systems should be implemented for each department, and as such, each process and subprocess of a transaction/activity that is recorded by the concerned employee should be systematically cross-checked or verified subsequently by other employees of that department or by other department where the transaction/activity flows through various departments and also by internal auditors so that fraud and pilferage can be ruled out completely. By doing this, all the departments will function professionally, and eventually, this will lead to the success of the entire organization's business.

STAGE 3: EXECUTION OF AGRI PROCESSES

- The risks here could be, not reaching the targets in terms of quantity or the produce being inferior to that of the benchmark quality or complete failure of that branch's processes or yield.

- These risks can be mitigated easily by strictly following all the protocols of the execution processes of each branch of agriculture in a timely manner. Also, all the resources, including financial and human, should be available at the required time for timely execution.

- A proactive approach and alternative plans in case of any problems or trouble should always be in place to mitigate any contingencies.

STAGE 4: POST HARVEST

Substage 1: STORAGE OF THE PRODUCE

The risk of not having adequate storage facilities might lead to distress sales and may incur losses particularly:

i. In the case of perishable goods

ii. In case prices fall due to "supply-demand" factors

So, we should be equipped with adequate storage facilities as required for each specific crop or any other produce of any branch of agriculture.

Substage 2: MARKETING OF THE PRODUCE

The risk of an inefficient marketing team or department directly affects our profits/revenue.

So, we need a strong and efficient marketing department that is result-oriented to reach targets within the time frames given.

The team should be robust to exploit internet technology and make our products reach its customers all over the globe.

Readers Note

Readers Note

CHAPTER 6

Implementation Modes to Make This Concept Successful

Agriculture is a field of unlimited possibilities.

— Anonymous

- We have spoken about another Green Revolution, which we hope will be perpetual. Revolution means a change from what is routine or already existing. It is human nature that people are averse to change. Besides this, we will face many challenges, expected and unexpected, and should face them head-on very courageously and with great trust.

- We should march ahead in a professional manner, with the help of a core team, plan ahead, anticipating contingencies, and be prepared to safeguard and manage them by always having alternative plans.

- We have taken care, as much as possible, to mitigate the risks and address the challenges in every stage of the complete cycle.

Besides this, our approach of choosing different agri processes in each profit center, based on soil and water health, is akin to that of portfolio investment management (a financial management concept), where money is invested in different schemes or stocks to diversify the risk. The risk of loss can be minimized or set off from the profits of the other investments.

- Success lies in strictly adhering to a professional and scientific approach. However, the people and the system that manage the entire show become critical for success. So let me explain how. Individual farmers cannot do things on their own because of many limitations—most of them do not have the required resources like capital. Also, a group of farmers or a community will not be able to succeed because of limitations like the pooling of huge capital, managing human resources, and many other reasons.

- Human greed for power, fame, and money will arise and there will be lots of conflicts in even small matters that will disturb and disrupt the entire functioning of the business. After a lot of observations and experience about existing systems and nature of human beings in business development and business destruction, I suggest that, in order to make this successful, it is possible, only if:

  1. Corporates go with a social-business concept

  2. State governments or the Central government go with a social-business concept

- The concept, as explained in this book, is about management and execution along the lines of the structure of corporate bodies.

- But the governments, either State or Central, can also play a role in adopting and implementing the concept across the country. But of late, we know that most of the public sector undertakings or government-aided companies are loss-making.

So, considering these data and information, one can be skeptical about Central Government action or success. However, I believe that the Central Government can also be successful if it adopts the discipline, structure, and systems of the armed forces. This is the only way—through disciplined and strict systems, rules and protocols, with a few modifications suitable to this idea—to drive success. The Central Government think tank can easily think innovatively to incorporate defense mechanisms into agriculture, too. Remember former prime minister, Lal Bahadur Shastri's, dream about our nation's prosperity with his slogan, *"Jai Jawan, Jai Kissan."* It is very clear that these two components are akin to two sides of the same coin. One side, the soldiers safeguard our country from enemies and the other side, the farmers safeguard from hunger while improving our economy.

- The government can invite public investment of up to 49% from the entire nation, get huge capital, and permit citizens to be owners of these government companies.

- The employees of these companies will have the privileged status of being government employees and also the psychological satisfaction of contributing to our motherland just as our soldiers do.

Readers Note

Readers Note

CHAPTER 7

Conclusion

Agriculture is the noblest of all alchemy; for it turns earth, and even manure, into gold, conferring upon its cultivator the additional rewards of health

— *Paul Chatfield*

- Any great idea, revolution, or transformation requires lots of courage, belief, and a never-give-up attitude to make it a reality. Of course, there are a lot of hurdles, and many people shall be pessimistic about the outcome; they believe it is impossible or impracticable. Obviously, it's a herculean task but it is very much possible. I remember Walt Disney's story, when he conceived the Disneyworld concept and told his friends and investors. They laughed at him and responded negatively asking him who would come to see the characters of Mickey Mouse, Donald Duck, etc.? But, today, The Walt Disney Company is one of the top 500 Fortune companies in the world and even The Facebook, Inc. now called as Meta Platforms, Inc. and Apple Inc. own some shares in it.

- What I want to convey is that some things look very unrealizable but are actually possible. In the case of Walt Disney, his unbreakable trust in himself and his idea was the only thing that mattered to make it a reality. But, here, I wish that collectively, many of the interested groups, experts, and think tanks of the government can modify this concept, which is in a nascent stage into a full-fledged, robust one so that it achieves the results envisaged in the book.

- Through the "Social-Business Concept", every citizen of India will get an opportunity to invest and grow their money. Besides, he will always be a co-owner of that agri company. The main intention is: "Let's every one of us grow together monetarily."

- A statutory regulatory authority—similar to SEBI in the case of financial security markets and the Real Estate Regulatory Authority (RERA) in the case of real estate markets—should be formed for the proper regulation of the entire processes of this concept so that it protects all the stakeholders in every way. For example, protecting the farmers' lands by providing leases and protecting investors by proper regulations.

- The government, on the other hand, has to encourage this idea by:

  ✓ Its implementation through a regulatory authority.

  ✓ Providing tax concessions in the initial 10 years to these agri companies/business organizations.

  ✓ Allowing 100% provision for free marketing of the surplus after apportioning the minimum percentage to be given to the government at a concessional rate or minimum support price (MSP) to provide food grains at subsidized prices to the entire nation.

- There are some other areas which are discussed below where they are to be compulsorily thought of to start or implement at least in the near future which has several benefits:

- ✓ **Agriculture Waste Management:** Agriculture waste in India is a growing concern due to the increasing demand for food and the limited resources available for proper management of waste. According to a report by the Central Pollution Control Board (CPCB), agricultural waste accounts for about 50% of India's total waste. The waste generated from activities such as crop residue, animal husbandry, and packaging materials is not properly managed, leading to environmental pollution, soil degradation, and health hazards. To address this issue, the Indian government has introduced several initiatives like composting, biogas production, and waste-to-energy systems. But more needs to be done to ensure sustainable waste management practices in the agricultural sector and through this idea we can surely achieve and convert waste into useful resources which can again generate huge revenues.

- ✓ **Earthworm Farming:** Earthworm farming is the practice of raising earthworms for commercial or recreational purposes. These worms can be raised in containers or in a natural environment and are often used to produce vermicompost, which is a nutrient-rich soil amendment that can be used in gardening. Earthworms can also be raised as a source of protein for humans and other animals, as well as for scientific and educational purposes. This is another area or agricultural activity which is revenue earning as well as helps making soil nutrient-rich.

- ✓ **Organic Farming:** Through this idea, there is a potential opportunity for the entire country to resort to organic farming whichever area of agriculture is suitable, has many benefits like:

  - ➢ **Environmental Benefits:**
    - Reduced chemical usage, which helps in preserving soil quality and preventing water contamination.

- Enhanced biodiversity and wildlife habitat, as organic farms promote the existence of various species.

- Carbon sequestration through healthier soil-management practices.

➢ **Health Benefits:**

- Organic foods are free from synthetic pesticides, herbicides, and GMOs, reducing health risks associated with chemical residues.

- Higher nutritional value in organic produce due to better soil quality.

➢ **Taste and Quality:**

- Organic produce is often considered to have superior taste and quality due to the absence of chemical additives.

➢ **Sustainability:**

- Organic kheti practices help to maintain long-term soil fertility and overall ecosystem health.

- Reduced reliance on fossil fuels as organic farms typically use less energy-intensive methods.

Of course, there are disadvantages as well like lower yields, higher costs, pest and disease management, transition period, market price fluctuations. All these can be addressed if this idea is adopted.

Readers Note

Readers Note

About the Author

Asheesh Seshadri is a practicing chartered accountant from Bengaluru. He spends most of his time thinking about life, philosophical matters, and innovative solutions for the problems faced by the people in our cities and country, for example, how to ease traffic congestion in Bengaluru, traffic safety to avoid accidents, how to solve the issue of drunken driving, solve the problems faced by old parents who have been sent old age homes so they can live happily for the rest of their lives, etc.

He has a philanthropical urge to contribute something worthy to this planet before he leaves the Earth—to make it a better place to live in. His approach is primarily socialistic, and he wishes to see an egalitarian society where there will be no gap between the haves and have-nots.

Asheesh Seshadri loves nature. He enjoys watching movies, reading books, and browsing social media and likes to play badminton and cricket.

www.ingramcontent.com/pod-product-compliance
Lightning Source LLC
Chambersburg PA
CBHW021130130726
47988CB00003B/1233